JAN
MORRIS

SCENES FROM
HAVIAN LIFE

D1324534

PENGUIN BOOKS

PENGUIN BOOKS

Published by the Penguin Group. Penguin Books Ltd, 27 Wrights Lane, London
W8 5TZ, England. Penguin Books USA Inc., 375 Hudson Street, New York,
New York 10014, USA. Penguin Books Australia Ltd, Ringwood, Victoria, Australia.
Penguin Books Canada Ltd, 10 Alcorn Avenue, Toronto, Ontario, Canada M4V 3B2.
Penguin Books (NZ) Ltd, 182 – 190 Wairau Road, Auckland 10, New Zealand · Penguin
Books Ltd, Registered Offices: Harmondsworth, Middlesex, England · This
extract is from *Last Letters from Hav*, by Jan Morris, first published by Viking 1985.
Published in Penguin Books 1986. This edition published 1996 · Copyright © Jan
Morris, 1985. All rights reserved · The moral right of the author has been asserted ·
Typeset by Rowland Phototypesetting Ltd, Bury St Edmunds, Suffolk. Printed in
England by Clays Ltd, St Ives plc · Except in the United States of America, this
book is sold subject to the condition that it shall not, by way of trade or otherwise,
be lent, re-sold, hired out, or otherwise circulated without the publisher's prior
consent in any form of binding or cover other than that in which it is published and
without a similar condition including this condition being imposed on the subsequent
purchaser · 10 9 8 7 6 5 4 3 2 1

SPRING — FLORA AND FAUNA — THE KRETEVS — THE DAY OF THE SNOW RASPBERRY — MY YELLOW HAT

Away beyond the Serai domes one can see the outlines of the western hills, where the Greeks built their pleasure-houses (so archaeologists assure us) and the Russians after them. When I came to this apartment they looked brown and melancholy, like so much else in Hav. Then, almost as I watched, they became perceptibly greener and happier. And yesterday, when I went out on to my balcony with my morning coffee, lo! they were a magical blush of pinks, blues and yellows.

'The spring of Hav!' announced Signora V emotionally. 'It is not,' she added, as she invariably adds, 'as it used to be' (in the Duce's day, I almost interjected), 'but still it is a kind of miracle. How wonderful nature is even in these distant places.'

I have acquired a car now. It is a 1971 Renault, and according to Fatima, who arranged the deal for me, it was once the tunnel pilot's transport. So in the afternoon I drove out to the hills to see the spring flowers for myself – swiftly through the wrinkled alleys of the Medina, along the fine big road the Russians built to take them to their pleasures, across the remains of the Spartan canal until the low hills rose on either side of me, speckled with neglected olive trees, decrepit villas and overgrown gardens. And the Signora was right: a miracle it was.

Every patch of broken ground, every gully, every broken-down Grand Duke's or Sturmbannführer's terrace was lyrically over-laid with flowers, half of them strange to me – flowers something like buttercups, but not quite, flowers very nearly bluebells, flowers not unrelated to asphodels or recognizably akin to primroses – and there were clambering plants with pink petals wandering everywhere, and up the gnarled trunks of the olive trees a sort of blossoming moss flourished. The combined scent of all these flowers, and many another herb, scrub and lichen no doubt, resolved itself into something peculiarly pun-gent, not unlike a sweet vinaigrette dressing, and overcome by this I lay out there flat on my back encouched in foliage. There was not a soul about. All those once-blithe houses, with their tattered awnings and their sagging pergolas, seemed to be utterly deserted. Far away over the canal the towers and gilded domes of Hav, the great grey-gold mass of the castle, looked from that bowered belvedere like a city of pure fiction.

It was absolutely silent there. I heard not a bird nor a cricket, was stung by no ant, bitten by no wandering gnat. Though Heaven knows Hav is no showplace of hygiene, I sometimes feel it to be almost antiseptically sterile. There seems to be a shortage of everyday bug, bird or rodent life. The other day I had lunch at the Athenaeum with Dr Borge, who likes to describe himself as Botanist, Anthropologist and Philosopher, and I put this point to him. 'You are right,' he said, as philo-sophers will, 'and you are wrong. You must realize that here in Hav our conditions of life are unusual. We are at once maritime and continental, Triassic and Jurassic, marsh and salt, lime and mud. Our fauna is not lavish, but as your Bard would say, it is true to ourselves!'

Such animal life as there is, sustained by this rare combination of soils, climates and geological origins, really is sufficiently peculiar. Once or twice in the greenery immediately below my balcony I have seen a strange little snouted creature snooping in the dusk, black, soft and low on the ground. This is the Hav mongoose, *Herpestes hav*, a mutation of the Indian mongoose brought in by the British to deal with the snakes; there is a stuffed specimen in the museum's little zoological collection, and it looks to me less like a mongoose than a kind of furry anteater.

Then the Hav hedgehog, *Erinaceus hav*, is odd too, since it is tailed, like a prickly armadillo, and the Hav terrier is like a little grey ball of wire wool, and I believe the troglodytes breed a pony of Mongolian origins on the foot-slopes of the escarpment. Some people say the so-called Abyssinian cat, now so fashionable in Europe and America, really came from Hav, in the kitbags of British soldiers; as it happened, the British garrison here was closed in the same year as the 1868 expedition to Magdala in Ethiopia, and it is suggested that some sharp characters among the returning soldiery conceived the idea of putting a new 'rare African cat' on the market. The modern Hav cat does not look much like the slinky patricians of Western fancy, but he is often distinguished by having extra claws on his front paws – the extra-toed cats which still swarm about Ernest Hemingway's house in Key West are claimed to have Hav ancestry.

Out on the marshes there are sheep, guarded by hangdog Arab shepherds (and hangdog they might well be, there in those dismal wastes). They are dull stringy creatures, but around them there often romp and scamper, as though in a state of permanent hilarious mockery, lithe and fleecy goats – so tirelessly jerky, springy and enterprising that from a distance, when you see one of those listless flocks like a stain on the flatlands, the goats prancing around it look like so many little devils.

I don't know what the British Resident's original cattle were like, when they arrived from England on the frigate *Octavia* in 1821, but the Hav cattle of today, who are all their descendants, would win no rosettes at county shows. Disconsolately munching the scrubby turf in their pastures at the foot of the escarpment, they seem to have gone badly to seed, having long pinched faces, heavy haunches and protruding midriffs. They have never been crossed with any other cattle, Dr Borge tells me, but I suspect the poor wizened cows among them would welcome the arrival, on some later *Octavia* perhaps, of a few lusty newcomers.

There are foxes, they say, on the escarpment. There are certainly rabbits. There used to be wolves; the last of them, allegedly shot by Count Kolchok himself on 4 June 1907, is mounted in the entrance hall of the Serai's North Block, looking a bit the worse for death. And only the other day, I read in *La Gazette*, a member of the Hav Zoological Society claimed to have spotted, while snake-hunting on the escarpment (where the mongoose never did thrive), a female Hav bear.

This rarest of European bears (*Ursus arctus hav*), which looks from pictures rather like a miniature grizzly, has repeatedly been declared extinct. Hunting the survivors was one of the fashionable pastimes of the *fin de siècle*: the King of Montenegro shot three or four, and you may see the skin of one still hanging in his wooden palace at home in Cetinje. As late as the 1930s, though the Tripartite Government had declared the animals protected, hunting parties used to go out from the Casino equipped with all the paraphernalia of safari, and sometimes claimed to have shot one: it was during one of these expeditions that Hemingway, so legend says, deliberately jogged the elbow of Count Ciano, thus saving the life of a bear offering a perfect shot upon the skyline ('You fool,' said the Count. 'You fascist,' said the writer).

Anyway, the bear apparently survives, nobody is quite sure how. The terrain of the escarpment is difficult and infertile, yet *Ursus arctus hav* has never, it seems, wandered over the crest into the easier flatlands of Anatolia, and has rarely been sighted in the Hav lowlands either. There were reports in the 1950s that a covey had somehow made themselves a lair within the escarpment tunnel – maintenance men reported seeing animal eyes glowing in alcoves as they went by on their trolleys, and for a time amateur zoologists went backwards and forwards on the train, to and from the frontier station, unavailingly hoping to catch a glimpse of them. More persistently, rumour has the Kretevs sheltering the bear in their warren of caves at the western end of the escarpment, either because they believe it to be holy, or just because they are fond of it. 'The 5 troglodytes,' Dr Borge told me learnedly, 'possess a special relationship with the animal world, not unlike I believe that of the ancient Minoans. You are aware of the Minoans? They venerated a monster, you will remember, within a labyrinth. Perhaps our Kretevs cherish other creatures within their caves?' It seemed improbable, I suggested, that only thirty-odd miles from the cafeteria of the Athenaeum such mysteries could persist. 'Ah,' said the young doctor, 'but you have not met the troglodytes. You do not know their obstinacy.'

Actually I have met some of them – I cultivate their acquaintance at the morning market, and have even struck up a sort of friendship with one of their more articulate stall-holders, who learnt some English as a merchant seaman, and whose name sounds to me like Brack. I concede, though, that of all the manifestations of nature in Hav, the Kretevs seem the most elusive. Talking the arcane unwritten language which, it is said, no foreign adult has ever mastered, crouched over their stalls with long tangled hair often half-bleached by the sun, their nondescript clothes set off by many bracelets and ear-rings, down at the market they seem to me like a race of gypsy Rastafarians, visiting the town from some other country altogether. Even Brack claims never to have set foot within the circuit of New Hav.

Yet they form a still living bridge between the city and its remotest origins. In the second or first centuries before Christ, the theory is, Celts from the Anatolian interior found their way to the edge of the great escarpment and saw before them, probably for the first time in their lives, the sea. So blue it seemed, we are told, so warm was the Mediterranean prospect, that they called the place simply 'Summer' – still *hav* or *haf* in the surviving Celtic languages of the West, just as 'Kretev' is thought to be etymologically related to the Welsh *crwydwyr*, wanderers. They were a continental people, though, a people of the land mass, and they never did settle upon the peninsula proper, forming instead troglodytic colonies in the raddled limestone caverns where their descendants still live. Their fellow-Celts of the interior presently evolved into the Galatians; and it was the poor Kretevs that St Paul had in mind when he wrote in his Epistle to the Galatians of 'your ignorant brethren living like conies in the rocks of the south'.

They are like strange familiars of the peninsula, and on one day in the year they perform a truly magical or mythological service to the city of Hav, whose foundation their presence here so long preceded, and from whose affairs they remain so generally remote. At dawn one morning, usually near the beginning of February, their gaily decorated pick-ups come storming into the morning market with far more than their usual gusto, blowing their horns fit to wake the Governor and out-blast Missakian's trumpet. They are not unexpected, since it happens every year, and the market throws itself immediately *en fête*. Every truck horn blows, every ship's siren hoots, and all the market people line the street to greet them. They are bringing, or rather one of the trucks is bringing, the first of the snow raspberries.

Almost the last too, for this supreme delicacy is to be found 7 only on three or four days of the year, when the early spring suns melt the last of the escarpment's winter snows. Like the dragon-fly, the snow raspberry is born only to die. It sprouts mushroom-like overnight, without warning, and by noonday it is gone. It grows only in shaded crannies of the limestone, and only the cave people know where to look for it, or are there to pick it anyway. Brack says he was first taken out to gather the snow raspberries when he was five years old.

The arrival of this fruit in Hav is like the arrival of the first Beaujolais Nouveau in Paris, or the first grouse of the season in London, but much more exciting than either. Nobody knows just when the snow raspberry will appear, and for a week or two around the end of January the morning market, they tell me, is in a high state of expectancy. Even Signor Biancheri has no prior claim to supplies – even he must await the day when, honking their celebratory way past the sleeping city, the troglodytes arrive in wild array with their small but priceless commodity. The cost of snow raspberries is phenomenal. Few people in Hav have ever tasted the fruit, and nobody outside Hav has ever tasted it at all, for if it is frozen it loses its savour altogether. I suppose the Kretevs themselves may eat a few, but otherwise almost every berry goes to the government (official receptions of the most important kind are often timed to coincide with the snow raspberry season), to Biancheri's kitchen at the Casino, or to the Chinese millionaires of Yuan Wen Kuo.

Signora Vattani claims to have tasted one in her youth, but I don't believe her for a moment. Fatima Yeğen says that the Kaiser, who was lucky enough to arrive in Hav at just the right moment, was given a basket of them to eat on his ride down the Staircase. Dr Borge claims to believe them imaginary – 'folk-loric, nothing more' – and says the Kaiser was probably palmed off with Syrian loganberries. But Armand ate one once, on 8 February 1929, when an international delegation from the League of Nations was feted at the Palace.

'Oh it was so funny, how you would have laughed! In came this single footman, as pompous as a monsignor, carrying a silver dish piled high with these snow raspberries. The biggest ones were on the top. I was just a young attaché, at the foot of the table almost. All down the room I heard the oohs and aahs, "wonderful", "*quelle expérience*", you know the kind of thing. But by the time the dish reached us young people at the end of the room, only a few shrivelled little red fruits remained for us. They tasted like very old dry cherries.

'My dear, you must not be shocked. We were very young and disrespectful. My dear friend Ulrich Helpmann, from the German Residency, who was the most disrespectful of us all, placed his precious raspberry on the palm of his hand and flicked it with his right forefinger – so! – across the table at me. It missed me altogether and hit the boiled shirt of the footman standing behind my chair. I mean to say, my dear, before you could blink your eye that man had scooped it off and eaten it. His one and only snow raspberry! He's probably boasting of it still.'

Anyway, as I was saying, spring is here. The shuttered colour-less Hav that greeted me has disappeared. The flowers are 9 blooming in the western hills, and everything else is tentatively blooming too. Even the functionaries of the Serai, when I went to have my permit stamped this morning, were emancipated into shirtsleeves. The sentries at the Palace are in white uniforms now, with smashing gold epaulettes, and the station café has set up its pavement tables on the edge of Pendeh Square, under the palms, beneath well-patched blue, white and green sunshades. I wore my yellow towelling hat from Australia to go to the Serai. '*Başında kavak yelleri esiyor*,' a passer-by said without pausing, which translated from the Hav Turkish means 'There is the springtime in your hat!'

THE ROOF-RACE

It is 5 May, the day of the Roof-Race. As the horse-race is to Siena, as the bull-running is to Pamplona, as Derby Day is to the English or even perhaps Bastille Day to the French, so the day of the Roof-Race is to the people of Hav.

It is not known for sure how this fascinating institution began, though there are plenty of plausible theories. The race was certainly being run in the sixteenth century, when Nicander Nucius described it in passing as 'a curious custom of these people'; and in 1810 Lady Hester Stanhope, the future 'Queen of Palmyra', was among the spectators: she vociferously demanded the right to take part herself, and was only dissuaded by her private physician, who said it would almost certainly be the end of her.

In later years the Russian aristocracy made a regular fête of it, people coming all the way from St Petersburg simply for the day, and lavish house-parties were organized in the villas of the western hills. Enormous stakes were wagered on the outcome; the winner, still covered with dust and sweat, was immediately taken to the Palace in the Governor's own carriage for a champagne breakfast and the presentation of the traditional golden goblet (paid for, by the way, out of an annual bequest administered by the Department of Wakfs).

Today gambling is theoretically illegal in Hav, but the goblet is still presented, more prosaically nowadays at the finishing line, and the winner remains one of the heroes of Hav for the rest of his life – several old men have been admiringly pointed out to me in the streets as Roof-Race winners of long ago. The race is so demanding that nobody over the age of twenty-five has ever run it – no woman at all yet – and only once in recorded history has it been won by the same runner twice; so that actually there is quite a community of winners still alive in Hav – the most senior extant, who owns the pleasure-garden on the Lazaretto, won the race in 1921.

The most familiar account of the race's origins is this. During a rising against the Ottoman Turks, soon after their occupation of Hav, a messenger was sent clandestinely from Cyprus to make contact with the patriotic leader Gamal Abdul Hussein, who was operating from a secret headquarters in the Medina. The messenger landed safely on the waterfront at midnight, but found every entrance to the Old City blocked, and every street patrolled by Turkish soldiers. Even as he stood there wondering how to get to Gamal, at his house behind the Grand Mosque, he was spotted by Turkish sentries and a hue and cry was raised; but far from retreating to his boat, whose crew anxiously awaited him in the darkness, without a second thought he leapt up to the ramparts of the Medina, and began running helter-skelter over the rooftops towards the mosque. Up clambered the soldiers after him, scores of them, and there began a wild chase among the chimney-pots and wind-towers; but desperately leaping over alleyways, slithering down gutters, swarming over eaves and balustrades, the messenger found his way through an upper window of Gamal's house, presented his message, and died there and then, as Hav legendary heroes must, of a cracked but indomitable heart.

Such is the popular version, the one that used to get into the guide-books – Baedeker, for instance, offered it in his *Mediterranean*, 1911, while adding that 'experienced travellers may prefer to view the tale with the usual reservations'. Magda has another version altogether, concerning the exploits of an Albanian prince, while Dr Borge regards the whole thing as pagan allegory, symbolic of summer's arrival, or possibly Christian, prefiguring the miracle of Pentecost. Most Havians, though, seem to accept the story of the messenger; and in my view, if it wasn't true in the first place, so many centuries of belief have made it true now.

The course is immediately demanding. It begins, as did the messenger's mission, with the scaling of the city wall, beside the Market Gate, and it entails a double circuit of the entire Medina, by a different route each time, involving jumps over more than thirty alleyways, culminating in a prodigious leap over the open space in the centre of the Great Bazaar, and ending desperately in a slither down the walls of the Castle Gate to the finish. The record time for the course is just under an hour, and officials are posted all over the rooftops, beneath red umbrellas like Turkish pashas themselves, to make sure there is no cheating.

Virtually all Hav turns out for this stupendous athletic event. All shops and government offices are closed for the day, and 13 almost the only person who cannot come to watch is Missakian the trumpeter, because it is his call from the castle rampart which is the signal for the start. In former times the race was run at midnight, as the messenger supposedly ran, but so many competitors died or were terribly injured, tripping over unseen projections, misjudging the width of lanes, that in 1882 the Russians decreed it should be run instead as dawn broke over the city – to the chagrin of those young bloods whose chief pleasure, if we are to believe Tolstoy, lay in seeing the splayed bodies falling through the street-lights to their deaths. But if it was well-ordered in Russian times, when Grand Duchesses came to watch, it is less so now: the race itself may be properly umpired and refereed, but the spectators, conveniently removed as they are from the actual course above their heads, are left absolutely uncontrolled. 'You are strong,' said Mahmoud, inviting me to join him at the great event, 'we will do the triple.'

This meant so positioning ourselves that we could see the three climactic moments of the race, one after the other – the start, the Bazaar Leap and the finish. For *aficionados* this is the *only* way to watch, and over the years dozens of ways of doing it have been devised. Some use bicycles to race around the outer circle of the walls. Some are alleged to know of passages through the city's cellars and sewers. Our system however would be simple: we would just barge our way, with several thousand others, down the clogged and excited streets from one site to the other.

Forty-two young men took part in the race this morning,

and when we hastened in the half-light to join the great crowd at the Market Gate, we found them flexing their muscles, stretching themselves and touching their toes in a long line below the city wall. Two were Chinese. One was black. One I recognized – he works at the Big Star garage, where I bought my car. One was Mahmoud's cousin Gabril, who works for the tramways company. Several wore red trunks to show that they had run the race before, in itself a mark of great distinction, and they were all heavily greased – a protection, Mahmoud said, against abrasions.

The eastern sky began to pale; the shape of the high wall revealed itself before us; from the mosque as we stood there in silence, came the call to prayer; and then from the distant castle heights sounded Missakian's trumpet. The very instant its last notes died those forty-two young men were scrabbling furiously up the stonework, finding a foothold here, a handhold there, pulling themselves up bump by bump, crack by crack, by routes which, like climbers' pitches, all have their long-familiar names and well-known characteristics. A few seconds – it cannot have been more – and they were all over the top and out of sight.

'Right,' said Mahmoud, 'quick, follow me,' and ruthlessly pushing and elbowing our way we struggled through the gate into the street that leads to the Great Bazaar in the very middle of the Medina. In sudden gusts and mighty sighs, as we progressed, we could hear spectators across the city greeting some spectacular jump, mourning some unfortunate slither – first to our right, then in front of us, then to our left, and presently behind our backs, as the runners finished their first lap. 'Quick, quick,' said Mahmoud to nobody in particular, and everyone else was saying it too – 'quick, only a few minutes now, we mustn't miss it, come along, dirleddy' – and at last we were beneath the vaulted arcade of the bazaar, lit only by shafts of sunlight through its roof-holes, shoving along its eastern axis until we found ourselves jammed with a few hundred others in the circular open space that is its apex.

We were just in time. Just as we got there we heard a wild padding of feet along the roofs above, and looking up we saw, *wham*, one flying brown body, then another, then a third, spreadeagled violently across the gap, rather like flying squirrels. One after the other they came, momentarily showed themselves in their frenzied leaps and vanished, and the crowd began to count them as they appeared – *dört, beş, altı, yedi* . . . Twenty-five came over in quick succession, then two more after a long pause, and then no more. 'Eight fallen,' said Mahmoud. 'I hope my cousin was not one' – but by then we had all begun to move off again, up the bazaar's north axis this time, to the Castle Gate. Now the crush was not so hectic. Everyone knew that the second half of the race was run much slower than the first – though the light was better by now, the terrible exertions had taken their toll. So we had time to conjecture, as we moved towards the finish line. Was that Majourian in the lead at the bazaar, or was it the formidable Cheng Lo? Who was the first Red Trunk? Had Ahmed Aziz fallen, one wondered – he was getting on a bit, after all . . . In a great sort of communal murmur we emerged from the bazaar, hurried down the Street of the Four Nomads, and passed through the Castle Gate into the square outside.

There the Governor was waiting, with the gold goblet on the table before him, attended by sundry worthies: the gendarmerie commander in his white drill and silver helmet, the chairman of the Assembly, the Catholic, Orthodox and Maronite bishops in their varied vestments, the Imam of the Grand Mosque, and many another less identifiable. There seemed to be a demonstration of some kind happening over by the Serai – a clutch of people holding banners and intermittently shouting: but the gendarmes were keeping them well away, and the dignitaries were not distracted. They did not have long to wait, anyway. Those spurts of wonder and commiseration grew closer and closer. The Governor joked benignly, as governors will, to ever-appreciative aides. The churchmen chatted ecumenically. The gendarmerie commander resolutely turned his back on the scuffles by the Serai. Splosh! like a loose sack of potatoes the first of the roof-runners, without more ado, suddenly fell, rather than jumped or even scrambled, down the sheer face of the gateway, to lie heaving, greased, bruised and bloody at the Governor's feet. Every few seconds then the others arrived, those that were still in the race. They simply let themselves drop from the gate-tower, plomp, like stunt-men playing corpses in western movies, to lie there at the bottom in crumpled heaps, or flat on their backs in absolute exhaustion.

It looked like a battlefield. The crowd cheered each new deposit, the dignitaries affably clapped. And when the winner had sufficiently recovered to receive his prize, the Governor, taking good care, I noticed, that none of the grease, blood or dust got on his suit, kissed him on both cheeks to rapturous cries of 'Bravo! Bravo the Victor!' rather as though we were all at the opera.

'Who won?' demanded Missakian, looking up from his beans and newspaper as we entered the station café for our breakfast. 'Izmic,' said Mahmoud. 'Izmic!' cried Missakian disgustedly, and picking up his trumpet he blew through it a rude unmusical noise.

When Marco Polo came to Hav in the thirteenth century, he was struck not so much by the wealth or power of the city, but by something unusual to its nature. 'This is a place of strange buildings and rites, not like other places.' Modern Hav is not perhaps exactly beautiful – it is too knocked about for that, has been infiltrated by too many shabby purlieus, frayed by too many reverses of fortune. But it does still possess some quality of fantasy, something almost frivolous despite its ancient purposes, and this is caused I think by its particular criss-cross mixture of architectural styles, which makes many of its buildings feel like exhibition structures, or aesthetic experiments. Add to this piquancy of mélange a certain flimsiness of construction – Hav bricks are small and slight, Hav roofs look lightly laid upon their joists – and the impression is given of a monumental but neglected folly, built by a sequence of playful potentates for their own amusement down the centuries.

The one Hav prospect that occasionally gets into picture books, having been painted by numberless artists of the T. Ramotsky school, is the view looking northward from the waterfront 19 towards the castle. Deposited here without warning out of the blue, you really might be at a loss to know where on this earth you were. To the right stands the hulk of the Fondaco, built of red brick brought from Venice, with its four squat corner towers, its machicolations, and its arcading half-filled now with hoardings and concrete walls. In the background, splendidly blocking the scene, the hill of the acropolis is crowned with the ruin of the castle, Beynac's keep mouldering at the summit, Saladin's gateway good as new below. To the left rise the walls of the Medina, protruded over by wind-towers, minarets and the upper floors of the huge merchant houses beside the bazaars.

And in the centre, seen across the busy traffic of the quay, is the official complex created by the Russians to celebrate their presence on this southern shore. The square itself, with its equestrian emperor in the centre, is said to be bigger than the Grand Square at Isfahan upon whose proportions the Arabs originally based it, and is bounded left and right by double lines of palm trees; between the eastern avenue the tramline runs, between the western is the gravel footpath along which Loti saw Nijinsky dance, originally preserved for Russian officials and their ladies, now a favourite public dalliance. The waterfront end of the square is marked by a line of bollards, placed there by the Venetians and made from captured Genoese guns; at the other end, where the winding path to the castle starts, there is a handsome double terrace, with urns and lions couchant on it, and in the middle a big circular fountain which, for all its dolphins, nymphs and bearded sea-gods, alas no longer founts.

Then to the east and west, more like pavilions than substantial buildings, rise the showy display pieces of Russian Hav, Serai on one side, station on the other. Their symbolism is extravagant, and entertaining. They represent Mediterranean Russia – the achievement at last of a dream as much aesthetic, or imaginative, as political. High above them tower the gilded onion domes, capped with gay devices, which instantly summon in the mind bitter steppes and snowy cities of the north – something of the sleigh and the fur hat, the samovar and perhaps the OGPU too – Mother Russia, at once smilingly and authoritatively embodied, here at the end of the railway line.

But below these bright globules, which somehow manage to be a little grim, as well as flashy, the architects Schröter and Huhn (who also designed the gigantic garrison cathedral at Tiflis, up the line) built in a very different allegory: for the tall arches and arcades below the domes, the gardens surrounding them, the inner courtyards and the long interior corridors are built in what architects Schröter and Huhn conceived as Southern Eclectic. Ogive arches in multi-coloured brick sustain that Slavic roofline, and there are high balconies with hoods, as in great houses of Syria, and even *mashrabiya* windows here and there. The courtyards are Alhambran, with prim patterns of orange trees; the tall shuttered windows of the wings might be in Amalfi or the old part of Nice.

Seen in the general rather than the particular, against the high silhouette of the castle hill, this ensemble really is rather spectacular, a little muted though its colours are now, a little   21 skew-whiff some of its shutters and rickety the less frequented of its balconies: and especially seen from the Electric Ferry, sliding quietly across the harbour, all those strange and disparate shapes, the towered severity of the Fondaco, the bright domes, the stark castle walls above, seem as they shift one against the other oddly temporary, as though one of these days the Grand Hav Exhibition must come to an end, and all its pavilions be dismantled.

The most celebrated architectural hybrid of Hav is the House of the Chinese Master in the Medina, directly outside the west entrance of the Great Bazaar. In the Middle Ages, when the Venetians were paramount upon the waterfront of Hav, the Chinese established a financial ascendancy in the city, and in 1432 the Amir was obliged to allow them a merchant headquarters actually within the Medina walls – hitherto they had been confined to their own settlement of Yuan Wen Kuo. They built it essentially in the glorious Ming style of the age, to plans said to have been sent from Beijing by the architect of the Qian Qing Gong, the Palace of Heavenly Purity in the Forbidden City; but they were subtle enough to make of it something specific to Hav. It is the westernmost of all the major buildings of Chinese architecture, and some say the finest Chinese construction west of the Gobi: discovering it for the first time out of the darkness of the Great Bazaar is perhaps the most astonishing aesthetic experience Hav can offer.

Imagine yourself jostling a way through those souks, shadowy, dusty, clamorous, argumentative, and approaching gradually, past charm-hawker and water-seller, blaring record shop and clatter of iron-smiths, the small yellow rectangle of sunshine that marks the end of the arcade. So great is the contrast of light that at first there is nothing to be distinguished but the dazzle itself; but as you get closer, and your eyes accustom themselves to the shine, you see resolving itself out there what seems to be a gigantic piece of black fretwork – multitudinous squares, triangles, circles and intersections, with daylight showing intricately through them. Is it some kind of huge screen? Is it something to do with the mosque, or an antique defence work? No: when you reach the end of the corridor at last, and step outside into the afternoon, you realize with delight that you have reached Qai Chen Bo, the House of the Chinese Master.

It *is* a house, and a very large one, but its inner chambers and offices, long since converted into a warren of tenements, are surrounded by a nine-sided mesh of elaborately worked black marble, forming in fact an endlessly spiralling sequence of balconies, but looking from the outside wonderfully lacy and insubstantial. The building is eleven storeys high, deliberately built a storey higher, so legend says, than any of the Arab structures of the city, and it is capped by a conical roof of green glazed tiles, heavily eaved and surrounded by pendent bobbles. It is reached by five wooden bridges over a nine-sided moat, once filled with fish and water-lilies, now only with rubbish: at each angle of the moat a separate small circular pool festers. The building is hemmed in nowadays by nondescript brick and concrete blocks, but still stands there sublimely individual 23 and entertaining – after five hundred years and more, much the liveliest building in Hav.

In 1927 Professor Jean-Claude Bourdin of the Académie française wrote a pamphlet about this building. All sorts of allusions, it seems, can be read into a construction that looks to the innocent eye no more than a splendid *jeu d'esprit*. The fundamental shape of the building is, of course, that of the pagoda, the most unmistakably Chinese of forms, with its wide eaves and its gently tapering flanks – the Arabs were to be left in no doubt, not for a moment, as to the nationality of the Master. In the five bridges there is apparently a direct reference to the five bridges over the Golden Water River in the Forbidden City, an allusion that would imply to the Chinese themselves, if hardly to anyone else, the presence here of the imperial authority. Then the moat itself, with its nine unblinking eye-pools, is claimed by Professor Bourdin to be a figure of the Lake of Sleepless Diligence, while the high corridor which bisects the ground floor of the building, west to east, is said to be exactly aligned upon Tian Tan, the Temple of the Heavens in Beijing. Finally, so Bourdin thinks, the whole edifice, so complex and deceptive, is a sophisticated architectural metaphor of the maze.

Well I'm sure he was right – he was a corresponding member of the Chinese Academy, too – but for me the House of the Chinese Master, whatever its subliminal purposes, is above all the most cheerful of follies. It is a building that makes nearly everyone, seeing it for the first time, laugh with pleasure, so droll is its posture there, so enchantingly delicate its construction, and so altogether unexpected its presence among the severities of medieval Islam. Here is what other visitors have written of it:

Pero Tafur, 1439: 'I have seen no building like this masterpiece, not in Rome, Venice or in Constantinople, and indeed I think it is the most remarkable and delightful of all buildings.'

Nicandur Nucius, 1546: 'The House of the Chinese Master at Hav is the merry wonder of all who see it.'

Anthony Jenkinson, 1558: 'In that part of the city where the Amir lives is a tall tower built by the Chinamen, exceeding ingenious and merry, so that had it not been for the severe scrutiny of the Mussulmans close by we would fain have burst out laughing at the spectacle.'

Alexander Kinglake, 1834: 'Do you remember when we were boys together we would make houses in the trees for our childish entertainments? Well, you must imagine all the tree-houses that ever were constructed pushed all on top of one another, and crowned with the wide straw hat that our good Mrs W used to wear to church on Sundays.'

Mark Twain, 1872: 'If I hadn't seen it with my own eyes I would have said it was more probably the House of the Chinese Teller of Tales – but there it was before me, and I could not have told a taller tale myself.'

D. H. Lawrence, 1922: 'A hideous thing. Restless, unsatisfied. And yet one could not help smiling at the vivid, brisk and out-flinging insolence of it.'

Robert Byron, 1927: 'Surrounded by the sombre piles of Islam, the House of the Chinese Master burst into our view in a flowering of spectacular eccentricity. It was impossible to leave the city after so brief a glimpse of this prodigy; sighing, we resolved to come back in the morning. "You don't want to see inside now?" nagged the wretched guide. "Alas, it is not allowed," said David at once. "We are Rosicrucians." '

But I will leave the last comment to Sigmund Freud, who lived for a time in modest lodgings on the eighth floor of the house: 'It is difficult for me to express how profound an effect this experience has had upon me. It is as though I have lived within the inmost cavity of a man's mind – and that the mind of a Chinese architect dead for five hundred years. No number of hours spent in analysis with my patients has brought me nearer to the sources of personality than the weeks I spent, all unthinking, in the House of the Chinese Master.'

I suppose you could say the very notion of New Hav is crossbred – critics certainly thought so when it was founded, and historians sometimes say so now. It was certainly a quixotic gesture, to choose this remote and inessential seaport for so advanced an experiment in internationalism. As to the construction of a brand-new city to house the concessionary areas, that was variously considered at the time as either an act of preposterous extravagance, or else a project nobly worthy of the age that was dawning after the war to end all wars.

An international committee of architects was invited to design New Hav, and the plan they drew up was patently consensus architecture, a little dull. What it lacks in genius, however, it makes up for in an unexpected and sometimes comic caprice of detail. The idea was to balance the roughly
circular walled city of the Arabs, on the western side of the

harbour, with a second walled city on the eastern side, leaving the Serai and the castle in between. The harbour gate of New Hav, opening on to a promenade upon the western quay, looks directly across the harbour to the Market Gate of the Medina. At the same time, the northern axis of the new city was to be aligned upon the castle hill, so that you could see the rock of the acropolis from the very middle of New Hav; but since this did not in the event prove possible in the city's geometrically tripartite form, the northern boulevard had to be twisted out of true, causing agonizing disputes between the French and the Italians, whose concessions it separated (in the end the Italians were compensated by being given possession of the promenade upon the harbour).

Everything else about New Hav is excessively symmetrical, and there is almost nothing that is not balanced by something else, and almost no vista that is not suitably closed. From the central Place des Nations, below my balcony, radiate the three dividing boulevards, Avenue de France northwards towards the Serai and the castle hill, Viale Roma westwards to the harbour, Unter den Südlinden eastwards towards nowhere in particular. The city was supposed to be a physical representation of the League's visionary initiative – a place of reconciliation and cooperation, of unity in variety. Its circular shape was meant to symbolize eternal peace, and each boulevard was planted with a different species of tree (planes, catalpas and ilexes) to express the joy of amicable difference.

The façades of Place and boulevards are all uniform – grandly neo-classical, in a Beaux-Arts style, arcaded at street level, mansard-roofed above – and they are marked with elegant tiled street signs, in four languages, contributed to this old haven of the Armenians by the Armenian Pottery in Jerusalem. But the liberty allowed to the powers to do what they like in their own quarters saves the place from sterile monumentality. Resolutely internationalist though they were, none of the three could resist the claims of patriotism when they were let loose on the side-streets, and there are few facets of French, Italian or German architecture that are not represented somewhere within the pattern of New Hav. There are mock-Bavarian inns. There is a music-hall (the Lux Palace) straight from Montmartre. There is a classic Fascist railway station, modelled on Milan's, which since no railway enters New Hav, was used as the Italian Post Office instead. If the French decided to build a cathedral, what else but a little Rheims would do? If the Germans wanted a Residenz, what but a small *Schloss*? Though everything is cracked and peeling now, it is all there to this day, Beaux-Arts to Bauhaus, neo-Imperial to late Nihilist (the Casa Frioli in the Italian quarter, a marvel of swirled concrete decorated with mosaics of glaring purple, is the least avoidable building in New Hav).

Two world-famous architects are represented. The glass-and-concrete Maison de la Culture in the French quarter, with its stilts and green cladding, is one of Le Corbusier's less inspired works: in it, between the wars, everyone from Colette to Malraux gave lectures on The Meaning of Frenchness or Allegory in Provençal Folk-Dance. More importantly, you may notice scattered fitfully through the German quarter a certain distinction of design in matters electrical: lamp-standards, light-switches, even a few antique electric fires and toasters all seem to obey some central directive of taste. This is because the German administration entrusted the power system of its quarter to the Berlin company AEG, and it was their great consultant architect Peter Behrens who, during a visit to Hav in 1925, drew up designs for the whole electrical network. Unfortunately he had no say in the power station, which had been built by the Russians and supplied the whole peninsula, but within the German quarter everything electrical was his – the bold transformer station, like a whale-back beside the Ostgatte, the powerful street-light pylons, the solid square switches of brown bakelite. Of course much of it is lost, but even now, so ubiquitous was Behrens's influence, there is a kind of subliminal strength to the style of the German quarter which is distributed, I like to think, directly through the frequently fused and multitudinously patched circuits of AEG-Hav.

For the rest, there is nothing of supreme quality. It is all a bit of a lark. All was done, one feels, even the Italian Post Office, in a spirit of genial optimism, elevated sometimes into parody. Architectural purists of the 1920s sneered mercilessly at New Hav, and Lutyens, invited to attend its formal opening in 1928, said privately that it reminded him of the ghost train on Brighton pier, so dizzy did it make him, and so often did damp objects slap him in the face.

But at least it possesses, as few such artificial towns do, an air of hopeful guilelessness. Just this once, it seems to say, just 29 for this moment, even our separate patriotisms are merely amusing. And most guilelessly amusing of all, to my mind, are the three arches by which each radial boulevard, as it debouches into the central Place, is ornamentally bridged. I can see all three from my terrace, if I lean out far enough. Close to the left a replica of the Bridge of Sighs ambiguously links our quarter with the French. Further round the Place, the Avenue de France is spanned by a squashed and potted representation of the towered bridge at Cahors. And opposite me stands an elevated Brandenburg Gate, splendid indeed when a No. 2 tram comes storming underneath with its rocking red trailer.

Armand thinks them all very silly, but he should not scorn Hav's follies, for the most gloriously ludicrous of them all was contributed by his own country. In those days it was an official French custom to distribute among Francophone communities across the world small iron replicas of the Eiffel Tower, still to be seen in places like Mauritius or Madagascar. It was thought improper, I suppose, to make such an offering to Tripartite Hav, so instead the French government presented the Conveyor Bridge which spans the harbour mouth beside the Iron Dog, perhaps ten miles south of the city centre, as a gesture of France's profound respect for the people and civilization of the peninsula. Only the French could build conveyor bridges – archetype was Lanvedin's magnificent Pont Transbordent at Marseilles – so its unmistakable outline on the finest site in Hav would be a perpetual reminder of French skill and generosity.

No matter that almost nobody wanted to cross the harbour

down there, or that the elaborate solution of a conveyor bridge was perfectly unnecessary anyway. The French mind was majestically made up, and to this day the bridge operates with the help of generous subsidies from Paris – besides being, thanks to its regular maintenance by French engineers, the most efficient piece of mechanism in Hav. Twelve times a day its platform, slung on steel wires from the girders high above, sets off in a gentle swaying motion across the harbour mouth, guided by a captain wearing a derivation of French naval uniform in his small wooden cabin in the middle. The pace is measured. The machinery is silent. A long chequered pennant streams from the cabin roof. To the north you can see the castle, rising on its rock above the city, to the south the Mediterranean Sea lies blue, green and flecked with foam. Below you, perhaps, a white salt ship slips elegantly out of the haven for Port Said and the Red Sea. In all Hav there is nothing much more foolish than the Conveyor Bridge – but nothing much grander, either!

I have been into the Palace, and met the Governor. A month after the Roof-Race the winner, by then assumed to have recovered from the ordeal, is honoured at a gubernatorial garden party, the Victor's Party, which is one of the great public occasions of the Hav year. It takes no great social clout to be invited, though Signora Vattani did look rather miffed when the big official envelope, stamped rather than embossed with the Governor's emblem (a Hav bear, rampant, holding a maze-mallet), plopped through our letter-box for me. Before the war, she said, she always used to go with her husband, but of course (with a sniff) everything was so different now . . .

Long before I reached the palace gates I could hear the thump of military music over the traffic of Pendeh Square, and the party was evidently in full swing by the time I presented my invitation to the smiling sentries, and had been stentoriously announced by the footman at the door of the central salon. The Governor was there to receive his guests. 'Dirleddy, I have heard so much of your presence here. You are welcome to Hav! Allow me to introduce our guest of honour and our hero, Irfan Izmic.' Izmic looked very unlike that heap of blotched, greased and bloody flesh which had dropped from the Castle Gate four weeks before. He was in a smart tropical suit now, his hair slicked, his moustache urbanely trimmed, in his lapel the red ribbon which winners of the great contest wear until the end of their days. 'Delighted dirleddy,' said he. 'Honoured to meet you,' said I, and so I was left, as one is left at garden parties the world over, hopefully to circulate.

I was happy enough to do so. It was a grand festivity to watch. Partly in the garden, partly in the salon beneath the chandeliers, the confused society of the peninsula milled, ambled or was clotted, offering for my contemplation a splendid cross-section of *Homo hav*. The noise was considerable. Not just the military band played, resplendent in white and scarlet in the little garden bandstand, but two other musical ensembles worked away indoors. In the blue drawing-room a piano quartet, three ladies and the urbane Chinese pianist I had last seen thumping jazz in Bar 1924, played café music with much careful turnings of pages and rhythmic noddings of heads. In the pink drawing-room a folk group of six girls and six men, dressed alike in straw hats and *gallabiyehs*, performed in penetrating quarter-tones upon flutes, lutes and tambourines.

Through these varying melodies the Havians shouted to each other in their several languages, so that as I wandered through the crowd I moved from Turkish to Arabic, from Italian to Chinese to surprisingly frequent enclaves of English – for as I have discovered from the Athenaeum, Hav intellectuals in particular love to talk English among themselves. Mahmoud was there and introduced me to his hitherto unrevealed wife, who looked like a very pretty deer, but seemed to speak no known language at all. Dr Borge was there and told me to ignore the folk-artists banging and fluting away in the other room, as they were pure phoneys – 'One of these evenings I'll take you to a place I know and let you hear the real thing.' Magda, in yellow, was accompanied by a handsome bearded black man, and who should be with Fatima (brown silk, helping herself to urchin mayonnaise from the buffet) but the stately figure of the tunnel pilot himself. 'I hear you have bought one of our old cars,' he said. 'A wise purchase. We keep them scrupulously.'

Presently the Governor adjourned with his guest of honour to a wide divan, covered with carpets in the Turkish way, which stood just within the french windows of the salon, looking out on to the garden. There they were joined by the Governor's wife and daughter, ample ladies both, in long white dresses and small tilted hats, who draped themselves side by side at the end of the divan, slightly separate from Izmic and His Excellency, and looked to me suggestively like odalisques. In twos and threes the citizenry took their turn to wait upon this court, and were greeted I noticed with varying degrees of condescension.

When for example athletic young men, with shy young wives, went over to grasp Izmic by the shoulder or pretend to rumple his hair, the Governor was all jollity, his ladies sweet with smiles. When elderly Turkish-looking gentlemen went, without their wives, sometimes the Governor actually rose to his feet to greet them, while his ladies adjusted their skirts and all but tidied their black hair. Others seemed less graciously received. I could not hear what was said, from my peregrinating distances, but I got the impression that sometimes the exchange of courtesies was curt. The Caliph's Wazir, though greeted by formal smiles, did not last long at the divan. A group of Greeks was all but waved away, and went off laughing rather rudely among themselves. And when Chimoun the Port Captain approached the presence with his svelte and predatory wife, I thought for a moment the Governor seemed a little nervous.

Magda and her black man, each holding a plate of langoustines, pressed me to a garden bench, in the shade of a fine old chestnut, from where I could view this intriguing pageant *in toto*. From there it all looked very colourful, very charming – the splash of crimson from the band in the corner, the bright dresses and gaudy hats, the wonderfully varied wandering wardrobe of kaftans, *gallabiyehs*, white uniforms, tight-buttoned suits and ecclesiastical headgear – and in the middle, intermittently revealed to us between the comings and goings of the guests, the Governor there on his divan, with his ladies and his champion, looking now so unmistakably Levantine that I almost expected him to pull his feet up under him and sit cross-legged on his rugs.

'I suppose you are thinking,' Magda remarked, 'what a pretty scene!' and her friend laughed cynically.

'Well it *is* a pretty scene,' I replied.

'You are so innocent,' Magda said, 'for a person of your age. You cannot have travelled much, I think. You sit here smiling around you as though it is a little show. You think it is all lobsters and urchins and nice music. Believe me it is much more than that.'

'You can say that again,' said her companion idiomatically. 35

'This is almost the only time in the whole year,' she went on, 'when all these people meet at the same time. Do you suppose they are here just to talk about the Roof-Race, or congratulate the Governor's daughter on her smart dress from Beirut? No, my friend, they're talking about very different things.'

'They're talking about money,' said the black man.

'Certainly,' said Magda, 'they're talking about money. And they're talking about power, and many other things too. They're not just here for fun. Look at them! Do they look as though they are having fun?'

They did actually, since half of them were stuffing urchins into their mouths, and many were laughing, and some were looking at the garden flowers, and others were deep in what seemed to be very absorbing gossip. But I saw what Magda meant. It was not exactly a *blithe* party. Currents I could not place, allusions I could not identify, seemed to loiter on the air. Separate little groups of people had assembled now, and appeared to have turned their backs on all the others. The longer I looked at the Governor the less he seemed like the benevolent figurehead of an idiosyncratic Mediterranean backwater, and the more like one of those spidery despots one reads about in old books of oriental travel, crouching there at the heart of his web.

'Well what d'you suppose they all *want*?' I asked.

'Ah,' said Magda sententiously, 'if we knew that, we would know the answer to life's riddles, wouldn't we?'

'That's for sure,' her friend added.

As I passed through the salon on my way out, having said my goodbyes to the divan ('Charmed, charmed,' murmured the two ladies, and the Governor bowed distractedly from the waist, being deep in talk with the Maronite archbishop), a man in well-cut sharkskin intercepted me. He was Mario Biancheri of the Casino. He had heard I was about, he said, and as we had friends in common in Venice, wondered if I would care to visit the Casino, which was difficult to enter without an introduction. 'You can drive out of course, but it's a terrible road – you really need four-wheel drive. But if you're prepared to get up early you could come with me in the launch one morning when we return from the market. We would see that you got home again. You would be amused? Very well, signora, it's fixed.

'By the way, did you enjoy the food? We did the catering. If you are planning to do any entertaining yourself we shall be delighted to help – we need not be as expensive as we look!' And so in the end I was seen off at the door of the palace, past the Circassian sentries, beneath the onion domes, away from the mysteries of that somewhat dream-like function, with a brisk quotation of sample prices – 'you prefer a sit-down meal? Certainly, certainly.' As I walked across the square the bands played on: thump of Sousa from the garden, 'Chanson d'amour' from the blue room, and a reedy wheeze and jangle of folk melody.

You may wonder what a maze-mallet is, such as appears in the paws of the bear on the Governor's emblem, and why a maze should be configured on the fretwork of the House of the Chinese Master. Forgive me. The maze is so universal a token of Hav, appears so often in legends and artistic references of all kinds, that one comes to take it for granted.

The idea of the maze has always been associated with Hav. The first reference to a Hav maze-maker comes in Pliny, who says the greatest master of the craft 'lived in the peninsula called by the people of those parts Hav, which some say means the place of summer, but others the place of confusions'. An ancient tradition says that the great labyrinth of Minoan Crete, in whose bowels the Minotaur lived, was made not by Daedalus, as the Greeks had it, but by the first and greatest of the Hav maze-makers, Avzar, who was kidnapped from the peninsula and blinded when his work was done: it is perhaps this remote fable that encouraged archaeologists, for many years, to suppose a Minoan connection in Hav, and to claim traces of Cretan design in the fragmentary remains of its acropolis.

Later it used to be said that the whole of the salt-flats,

with their mesh of channels, conduits and drying-basins, were originally nothing more than a gigantic maze, fulfilling some obscure ritual purpose, and of course it has been repeatedly suggested that the caves of the Kretevs, which have never been scientifically explored, are not really caves at all, but only the visible entrances of an artificial labyrinth riddling the whole escarpment. How proper it seemed to Russian romantics, that the Hav tunnel should spiral upon itself so mazily within the limestone mass!

There is an innocuous little maze of hedges and love-seats in the Governor's garden, and one or two are rumoured to be hidden within the courtyard walls of houses in the Medina. Otherwise there are no Hav mazes extant, and for that matter none historically confirmable from the past. Yet the spirit of the maze has always fascinated the people of Hav, and the tokens of the maze-maker, as they have been fancifully transmitted down the ages, are inescapable in the iconography of the city: the mallet, with which Avzar at the beginning of time beat his iron labyrinth into shape, the honeycomb which is seen as a natural type of the maze, the bull-horns which are doubtless a vestige of the supposed Minoan link.

Some scholars go further, and say that the conception of the maze has profoundly affected the very psyche of Hav. It certainly seems true that if there is one constant factor binding the artistic and creative centuries together, it is an idiom of the impenetrable. The writers, artists and musicians of this place, though they have included few native geniuses, have seldom been obvious or conventional. They have loved the opaque more than the specific, the intuitive more than the rational. Pliny said they wrote in riddles, and declared their sculptures to be like nothing so much as lumps of coral. Manet on the other hand, visiting Hav as a young man in 1858, wrote to his mother: 'I feel so much at home in this city, among these people, whose vision is so much less harsh than that of people in France, and whose art looks as though it has been gently smudged by rain, or blurred by wood-smoke.'

For myself I suspect this lack of edge has nothing to do with mazes, but is a result of Hav's ceaseless cross-fertilization down the centuries. Hardly has one manner of thought, school of art, been absorbed than it is overlaid by another, and the result, as Manet saw, is a general sense of intellectual and artistic pointill-ism – nothing exact, nothing absolute, for better or for worse. You can see it at the museum in the folk-art of the peninsula, which is a heady muddle of motifs eastern and western, realist and symbolical, practical and mystically unexplained; and you can see it all around you in the architecture.

The Arab buildings of Hav, for instance, were less purely Arab than any others of their age. It was not just a matter of incorporating classical masonries into their buildings, as often happened elsewhere: the Corinthian columns of Hav's Grand Mosque were made by the Arabs themselves, and on many of the tall merchant houses of the Medina you may see classical pilasters and even architraves, besides innumerable eaves and marble embellishments derived from the House of the Chinese Master. The one great Chinese building in the peninsula is a

mish-mash of architectural allusions. The British built their

Residency as if they were in India. And we have seen already with what adaptive flair architects Schröter and Huhn, when the time came, mixed their metaphors of Hav. It is the way of the place – rivers of history! You remember the quotation?

Very early in Hav's history the arts began to show symptoms of cultural confusion. 'The language of these people,' Marco Polo wrote, 'which is generally that of the Turks, contains also words and phrases of unknown origin, peculiar to hear.' They were, linguists have only recently come to realize, words of the troglodytic language, a fragile offshoot of the Celtic.

The earliest known poet of Hav was the Arab Rahman ibn Muhammed, 'The Song-Bird', who lived in the thirteenth century: in his work occur words, inflexions, ideas and even techniques (including the alliterative device called *cynghanedd*) which seem to show that in those days a Celtic poetic tradition was still very much alive in this peninsula. It has even been lately suggested that Rahman may have been in touch with his contemporary on the far side of Europe, the Welsh lyric bard Dafydd ap Gwilym. Here in Professor Morris David's translation are some lines from the Song-Bird's poem 'The Grotto':

> Ah, what need have we of mosque
> Or learned imam,
> When into the garden of our delights
> Flies the sweet dove of Allah's mercy
> With her call to prayer?

And here in my own translation is part of Dafydd ap Gwilym's poem 'Offeren y Llwyn', 'The Woodland Mass':

There was nothing there, by great God
Anything but gold for the chancel roof . . .
And the eloquent slim nightingale,
From the corner of the grove nearby,
Wandering poetess of the valley, rang to the multitude
The Sanctus bell, clear its trill,
And raised the Host
As far as the sky . . .

Coincidence? Or perhaps, more probably than actual communication between the two poets, some empathy of temperament and tradition. Celtic words had disappeared from the Hav poetic vocabulary by the seventeenth century, but still the poet Gamal Misri was writing of the natural world in a way quite unknown among other Muslim poets of the day, and dealing with religious matters in idioms astonishingly close to those of his contemporaries far away on the western Celtic fringe – idioms that would have cost him dear in Egypt, Persia or Iraq. This is his startling evocation of the Attributes of Allah, again in David's version:

He can see as doth the Telescope, to the furthest Stars.
He knows of the ways of man as the Compass knoweth the Pole.
He doth create Gold from Dross as doth the Alchemist,
And as the great Advocate doth argue for us before the Courts of
    Eternity . . .

Visual artists, too, even in the great days of Islamic Hav, did not hesitate to risk the disapproval of the faithful by painting living portraits – not simply stylized representations, such as you find in Persian miniatures, but formal portraits of real people, sitting to be painted as they would in the west. The so-called Hav-Venetian school of painting, which flourished throughout the sixteenth century, was unique, producing the only such genre in the Islamic world, and there are no examples of its work outside Hav. Even in the city they are very rare. A few are thought to be in private hands, but the only specimens on public display are five hanging in the former chapel of the Palace, which is open to the public at weekends. They are very strange. Large formal oil-paintings of merchants and their wives, dressed in the Venetian style but looking unmistakably Havian with their rather Mongol cheeks and hard staring eyes, their painters are unknown, and they are signed simply with illegible ciphers and the Islamic date. They are hardly, I think, great works of art. They look as though they have been painted by not terribly gifted oriental pupils at the atelier of Veronese, say, being very rich in colour and detail (pet terriers, mirrors, the House of the Chinese Master in one background, the harbour islands in another) but queerly lifeless in effect. I suspect myself that the artists were Chinese, for they remind me of paintings done for European clients in Canton in the eighteenth century, though their technique is far more sophisticated and their subjects are altogether more sumptuous. The Havians are immensely proud of them, and forbid their copying or reproduction – but that may be only a relic of the days when their very existence was kept a secret, lest Islamic zealots harm them.

I really do not think Havians excel at the musical art. They are adept enough at western forms, and addicted to Arabic pop, 43 but the indigenous kinds seem to me less than thrilling. Dr Borge was as good as his word, and took me last week to the 'place he knew', which turned out to be a dark café in one of those morose unpaved streets of the Balad, between the railway line and the salt-flats. Here, he said, the very best of Hav folk-music was to be heard. The night we went the performers were a particular kind of ensemble called *hamshak*, 'sable', because they specialized in elegiac music, and this made for a melancholy evening. They were all men, dressed in hooded monk-like cloaks supposed to be derived from the habits of Capuchin confessors who came here with the Crusaders. Their instruments were rather like those of the folk-music group at the Victor's Party, only more so: reedier, wheezier, janglier still, and given extra density by two drummers beating drums made of furry animal skins. ('Hav bear skins,' said Dr Borge – 'no, I am only joking'). We drank beer, we ate grilled fish with our fingers, and through the sombre light of the place the music beat at us. Sometimes, apparently without pattern, one or another of the musicians broke into a sad falsetto refrain ('reminiscent isn't it,' said the young doctor, 'of *cante hondo*?'). Sometimes, in the Arab way, the music suddenly stopped altogether and there was a moment of utter silence before the whole band erupted once more in climactic unison.

It was more interesting than enjoyable. It *was* rather like *cante hondo*, having sprung I suppose from the same musical roots. But the clatter of the tambourines and the clash of the cymbals reminded me irresistibly of Chinese music, such as one endures during the long awful hours of the Beijing Opera, while the plaintive notes of the flutes seem to come from some other culture entirely. Could it be, I wondered, that in Hav music, as in Hav medieval poetry, some dim Celtic memory is at work? Anything was possible, the Philosopher said; and when after the performance I put the same question to the band leader, a suitably cadaverous man with an Abraham Lincoln beard, his eyes lit up in a visionary way. 'Often I feel it,' he said, 'like something very cold out of the long ages' – a sufficiently convincing phrase, I thought, to catch his inspiration's meaning.

Out of the long ages certainly comes the genius of Avzar Melchik, the best-known Hav writer of the twentieth century, whose personality I can most properly use to cap this brief digression into criticism. If there is nothing overtly Celtic in his work, there is much that is undeniably mazy – even the given name he adopted, you may notice, is that of the great maze-man of legend.

Melchik, who died in 1955 (the year in which he was tipped as a likely rival to Haldór Laxness for the Nobel Literature Prize), wrote in Turkish and in French, and sometimes in both at the same time, alternating passages and even sentences between the languages. He was never in the least Europeanized, though – Armand dismisses him as a mere provincial – and his novels, if you can call them novels, are all set in Hav. They are powerful evocations of the place, through which there wander insubstantial characters, figures of gossamer, drifting for ever through the Old City's alleys or along the waterfront. Melchik so detested the invention of New Hav that he refused to recognize its existence in his art, and though his stories are set in the 1940s and 1950s, the Hav that they inhabit is essentially Count Kolchok's Hav, giving them all a haunting sense of overlap.

There is no doubt that Melchik was obsessed by the idea of the maze. Every one of his books is really its diagram. But in his most famous work, and the only one widely known in the West, he turns the conception inside out. *Bağlılık* ('Dependence') is the tale of a woman whose life, very gently and allusively described, is a perpetual search not for clarity but for complexity. She feels herself to be vapidly self-evident, her circumstances banal, and so she deliberately sets out to entangle herself. But when at last she feels she is released from her simplicities – has reached the centre of the maze in fact – she finds to her despair that her last state is more prosaic than her first.

Soon after finishing *Bağlılık* Melchik died. He was unmarried, and lived a life of supreme simplicity himself in a small wooden house, hardly more than a hut, on the edge of the Balad. It is now kept up as a little shrine, with the writer's pens still on his desk, his coat still hanging behind the door, and beside the china wash-basin, for all the world as though he has just been called into another room, the copy of Pascal's *Pensées* which he is said to have been reading on the last day of his life. An elderly woman acts as caretaker, paid by the Athenaeum, and told me when I visited the house that she felt the shade of Melchik ever-present there. 'When I make myself a cup of coffee in the kitchen, I often feel I should make one for him too.'

'And do you like this ghost?'

She thought for a moment before she replied. 'Have you been to his grave?' she asked. 'Perhaps that will answer the question for you.'

So I went there. Melchik was a Maronite Christian, and he is buried in the Maronite cemetery behind the power station. His grave is not hard to find – it stands all by itself at the northern corner within a hedge of prickly pears. You can see nothing of it, though, so formidable is this surrounding barrier, until you are within a few feet: and then you find it to be, not a slab, or a cross, or an obelisk, but a twisted mass of iron, like a half-unravelled ball of metallic wool, mounted on a stone slab with the single word MELCHIK just visible within the tangle. He designed it himself.

I saw what the caretaker meant. Could one exactly *like* such a spirit? Nothing, I thought, so cut-and-dried: but even there, all the same, where Melchik was represented only by those crude bold letters within the meshed and worried metal, I felt his presence burning.

Few places, I must say, honour their emblems more loyally than Hav honours its generic and imaginary maze. This city may not look especially labyrinthine, but behind its façades, I am coming to realize, beneath its surfaces bold, bland or comical, there lie a myriad passages unrevealed. Perhaps even the subterranean short cuts of the Roof-Race enthusiasts are only allegorical really!

Of course all cities have their hidden themes and influences

– New York has its Mob, Rome its Christian Democrats, London its Old Boy Network, Singapore its Triads, Dublin its Republican Army, all working away there, out of sight and generally out of thought, to determine the character of the place. The unseen forms of Hav, though, seem to me harder to define than any, so vague are they, so insidious, and I find it difficult to enunciate the feeling this is beginning to leave in my mind. It is a tantalizing and disquieting sensation. It is rather like the taste you get in the butter, if it has been close to other foods in the refrigerator; or like the dark calculating look that cats sometimes give you; or the sudden silence that falls when you walk into a room where they are talking about you; or like one of those threadbare exhausting dreams that have you groping through an impenetrable tangle of time, space and meaning, looking for your car keys.

A VISIT TO THE TROGLODYTES

All this time (it may have crossed your mind) and I still had not clambered the escarpment to the cave-homes of the Kretevs, the most compelling of all the Havians! I wonder why? Sometimes I was afraid of disillusionment, I suppose, in this city of reappraisals. Sometimes I reasoned that I should end with the beginning, and keep those atavists for my last letter. And sometimes I felt that, what with the Cathars, and the British Agency's radio masts, and the peculiar island Greeks, I was surfeited with enigma. But I kept in touch with Brack, and at the market the other day he beckoned me over to his stall. He said that if I wanted to come to Palast (which is, so far as I can make out, more or less what the troglodytes themselves call their village) I had better come that very day – if I brought my car I could join the market convoy when it went home in the afternoon. Trouble was brewing in Hav, he said, bad trouble, and it might be my only chance. He shook his head in a sorrowful way, and his ear-rings glinted among his dreadlocks. So at three o'clock – sharp! – I drove down to the truck park, and found the Kretev pick-ups all ready to go. Brack leant from his cab and gestured me to follow him. The other drivers, starting up their engines, stared at me blankly.

Trouble? All seemed peaceful, as we drove along the edge of the Balad and into the salt-flats. The old slave-settlement 49 looked just as listless as it had when I first saw it, so dim-lit and arid, through the windows of the Mediterranean Express. Some small boys were playing football on the waste ground beside the windmills. Away to the west I thought I could distinguish Anna's villa, in the flank of the hills, and imagined her settling down, now as always, to tea, petits fours, and her current novel (she is very fond of thrillers). The usual lonely figures were labouring in the white waste of the salt-pans, and now and then one of the big salt-trucks rumbled by on its way to the docks.

But just as we left the marshes and approached the first rise of the escarpment, Brack leant out of his window again and pointed to something in the sky behind us: and there were two black aircraft, flying very low and very fast out of the sea – except for the passing airliners, the first I had ever seen over Hav.

In the event I did not have to clamber to the caves, for one can drive all the way. It is a rough, steep and awkward track though, and most of the Kretevs left their trucks at a parking place at the foot of the escarpment, piling vigorously into the back of Brack's pick-up and into my Renault. Thus I found myself squeezed tight in my seat by troglodytes when I drove at last into the shaly centre of Palast – which, like so many things in Hav, was not as I expected it to be.

I had supposed it something like the well-known cave settlements of Cappadocia, whose people inhabit queer white cones of rock protruding from the volcanic surface. But Palast is much more like the gypsy colony of Sacramonte in Spain, or perhaps those eerie towns of cave-tombs that one finds in Sicily, which is to say that it is a township of rock-dwellings strung out on both sides of a cleft in the face of the escarpment. Wherever I looked I could see them, some in clusters of five or six, some all alone, some at ground level, some approached by steps in the rock, or ladders, some apparently altogether inaccessible high in the cliff face. Many had tubs of greenery outside, or flags of bright colours, and some had whitewashed surrounds to their entrances, like picture frames.

The flat floor of the ravine was evidently common ground, with a row of wells in the middle. Shambled cars, not unlike my own, were parked at random around it, stocky ponies wandered apparently at liberty, hens scooted away from my wheels. Out of some of the cave doors, which were mostly screened with red and yellow bead curtains, heads poked to see us come – a woman with a pan in her hand, an old man smoking a cigar, half a dozen boys and girls who, spotting my unfamiliar vehicle, came tumbling out to meet us. Soon I was sitting at a scrubbed table in Brack's own ground-floor cave, drinking hot sweet tea with his young wife, whose name sounded like Tiya, and being introduced to an apparently numberless stream of neighbours, of all ages, who came pressing into the cave.

When I say I was being introduced, it was generally in a kind of dumb show. Some of the men spoke Turkish, some a little Arab or French, but the women spoke only Kretev. We shook hands solemnly, exchanged names and inspected each other's clothes. Here I was at a disadvantage. I was wearing 51 jeans, a tennis shirt and my yellow Australian hat, rather less spring-like now after so much bleaching by the suns of Hav. They on the other hand were distinctly not wearing the jumbled neo-European hand-downs I had expected from the appearance of their market men on the job; on the contrary, they were in vivid reds and yellows, like the door curtains, the women in fine flowing gypsy skirts, the men in blazing shirts over which their long tangled hair fell to great effect. They jammed the table all around me and I felt their keen unsmiling eyes concentrated hard, analysing my every gesture, my every response. Their faces were very brown, and they smelled of a musky scent. Sometimes their ear-rings and bangles tinkled. Whenever I was not talking they fell into a hushed but animated conversation among themselves.

'They want to know,' Brack told me, 'what you think of our caves.' The caves seemed fine to me, if his own was anything to go by. It was far more than a cave really, being four or five whitewashed rooms, three with windows opening on to the common ground outside, furnished in a high-flown romantic mode, tapestry chair-covers and mahogany sideboards, and lit by electric lights beneath flowered glass lampshades definitely not designed by Peter Behrens of AEG. Everything was brilliantly clean: it reminded me of a Welsh farmhouse, not least the miscellaneous mementoes of Brack's naval service that were neatly displayed in the glass-fronted corner cupboard. The water, I was told, had to be drawn from the wells, but the electricity came from the Kretevs' own generator.

It all seemed fine, I said. But was there any truth in the

rumour that the caves really joined together, forming a secret labyrinth inside the escarpment? They did not, as I expected, laugh at this. They talked quite earnestly among themselves before Brack interpreted. 'We don't think so,' he said, 'we have never found one, but our people have always maintained that there is one great tunnel in the mountain behind us, and they say a great leader of our people long ago sleeps in there, and if we are ever in danger he will awake from sleep with his warriors and come out to help us. That is the story.' What about the treasures of the old Kretevs, the goblets, the golden horses, which I had been told from time to time were picked up on the escarpment? Then they *did* laugh. No such luck, they said, and when many years before some archaeologists had excavated the barrow-tombs down in the salt-flats, which were said to be the graves of primeval Kretevs, they found nothing inside but old bits of natural rock, placed there, it was supposed, because they bore some resemblance to human faces.

There was a thumping noise outside, and a rumble, and with a flicker the lights came on. Then we had supper. Everyone stayed for it, even the children who had been hanging about their parents' legs or staring at me from the doorway. It was goat stew in a huge tureen, with fibrous bread that Tiya had made. We helped ourselves with a wooden spoon and ate out of a variety of china bowls, some brought in from neighbouring caves because there were too few to go round. We never stopped talking. We talked about the origins of the Kretevs ('we came out of the earth, with horses'). We talked about the snow raspberries (not so plentiful as they used to be, but then that made for higher prices). We talked about Kretev art ('they do not understand your question') and Kretev religion ('we do not talk about that'). We talked about earning a living (their goat-herds, their market-gardens, their grassland where the cattle grazed). We talked about their language, but inconclusively; every now and then I heard words which seemed vaguely familiar to me, but when I asked their meaning no bells were rung, and when I invited the Kretevs to count up to ten for me, hoping to recognize some Celtic affinities, I recognized not a single numeral. What were their names again? Around the room we went, but not a name seemed anything but totally alien – Projo (I write as I heard them), Daraj, Stilts, what sounded improbably like Hammerhead. They had no surnames, they said: just the one name each, that was all. They needed no more. They were Kretevs!

Not Havians, I laughed, and that brought us to the condition of the city which lay, feeling a thousand miles away, through the string-bead curtains of that cave, and down the gully across the salt-flats. What was happening down there? What was the vague feeling of malaise or conspiracy that seemed to be gathering like a cloud over the city? Who slashed the paintings in the palace chapel? Most ominously of all, what were those black aircraft we had seen on the way up? None of them knew. 'Bad things,' said Brack, 'that's all we know.' Were they worried? They did not seem to be. 'We are here, it is there.' Besides, they had no high opinion of life down on the peninsula. 'Do you not know,' said Brack, speaking for himself now, 'what sort of people they are? Each talks behind the other. Have you not discovered? Hav is never how it says. So . . .' He splayed his hands in a gesture of indifference, and all around the table the brown faces gravely nodded, or leaned backwards with a sigh. 'We are here, it is there.'

And did they, I asked, ever see a Hav bear these days? Supper was over by then, and we were drinking out of a cheerful assortment of tumblers, cups and souvenir mugs from Port Said the Kretevs' own liqueur, made from the little purple bilberries which abound on the upper slopes of the escarpment, and alleged to cause hallucinations, like the magic mushroom, if you drink too much of it. There was silence for a moment. Somebody made a joke and raised a laugh. They talked among themselves in undertones. Then, 'Come on,' said Brack, taking a torch from the mantelpiece, 'come with us.' Out we trooped into the moonlit night, the whole company of us, some people scattering to their own caves to pick up torches; and so in an easy straggle, fifteen or twenty of us I suppose, torch beams wavering everywhere up the ravine, we walked up the gravel track towards the face of the escarpment. Above us the rocks rose grey and blank; all around the lights of the cave-dwellers twinkled; low in the sky, across the flatlands, a half-moon was rising. Through some of the open cave-doors I could see the flickering screens of TV sets, and discordant snatches of music reached up stereophonically from all sides. The engine of the generator rhythmically thumped.

It was a stiff climb that Brack led us in the darkness, off the sloping floor of the ravine, up a winding goat path, very steep, which took us high up the escarpment bluff, until those lights of Palast were far below us, the music had faded, and only the beat of the generator still sounded. The Kretevs, though considerably more out of breath than the hermits of the eastern hills, were not dismayed. They were full of bilberry juice, like me. The women merrily hitched up their skirts, the men flashed their torches here and there, they laughed and chatted all the way. They seemed in their element, in the dark, on the mountain face, out there in the terrain of *Ursus hav* and the snow raspberries.

Quite suddenly, almost as though it had been switched off, we could no longer hear the noise of the generator. 'When we hear the silence,' said Brack, 'we know we are there' – for at the very same moment we crossed a small rock ridge and found ourselves in a dark gully, with a big cave mouth at the end of it. The Kretevs stopped their chatter and turned their torches off. 'We must be quiet now,' whispered Brack. In silence we walked up the gully, and I became aware as we neared the cave of a strange smell: a thick, warm, furry, licked smell, with a touch of that muskiness that I had noticed on the Kretevs themselves – an enormously old smell, I thought, which seemed to come from the very heart of the mountain itself.

We entered the cave in a shuffling gaggle, like pilgrims, guided only by Brack's torch. It was not at all damp in there. On the contrary, it felt quite particularly dry, like a hayloft, and there was no shine of vapour on its walls, or chill in its air. The further we went, the stronger that smell became, and the quieter grew the Kretevs, until they walked so silently, on tip-toe it seemed, that all I could hear was their breathing in the darkness. Nobody spoke. Brack's torch shone steadily ahead of us. The passage became narrower and lower, so that we had to bend almost double to get through, and then opened out once more into what appeared to be a very large low chamber, its atmosphere almost opaque, it seemed to me, with that warmth and must and furriness. Brack shone his torch around the chamber: and there were the bears.

At first (though by now I knew of course what to expect) I did not realize they were bears. They looked just like piles of old rugs, heaped on top of one another, like the discarded stock of a carpet-seller. They lay in heaps around the walls of the chamber, motionless. But the Kretevs began to make a noise then, a sort of soothing caressing noise, something between singing and sighing, and all around the cave I heard a stirring and rustling – grunts, pants, heavings. When Brack shone his torch around again, everywhere I could see big brown heads raised from those huddles, and bright green eyes staring back at us out of the shadows. The bears were not in the least hostile, or frightened. One or two rolled their heads over sleepily, like cats, burying them in their paws. One was caught by the torch-light in the middle of a yawn. None bothered to get to its feet, and as the Kretevs ended their crooning and we stole away down the passage again, bumping into one another awkwardly in the silence, I could hear those animals settling down to sleep again in their soft and fusty privacy.

When we reached the open air again the moon was glistening upon the salt-flats below, and the Kretevs burst once more 57 into laughter and conversation. They seemed refreshed and reassured by their visit to the bears, and gave me the impression that they would one and all sleep like logs that night, in their own scattered caverns of the hillside.

I did too, in my sleeping-bag in the cool back room of Tiya's cave, and got up in the morning in time to say goodbye to the market men before the dawn broke. The goat-herds and gardeners were already climbing up the ravine. 'Come back again,' said Brack as he shook my hand, but I felt I never would. 'Look after yourselves,' I said in return. When I left Palast myself, a couple of hours later, all the young men had gone, and there were only women, children and old men to see me off. Their farewell was rather formal. They stood there still and silent, even the children, as I turned on the engine and started the Renault's reluctant ignition (not what it was when the tunnel pilots had it). 'Goodbye,' I said, 'goodbye.' They smiled their wistful smiles, and raised their hands uncertainly.

PENGUIN 60s

PENGUIN 60s

READ MORE IN PENGUIN

For complete information about books available from Penguin and how to order them, please write to us at the appropriate address below. Please note that for copyright reasons the selection of books varies from country to country.

IN THE UNITED KINGDOM: Please write to *Dept. EP, Penguin Books Ltd, Bath Road, Harmondsworth, Middlesex UB7 0DA.*

IN THE UNITED STATES: Please write to *Consumer Sales, Penguin USA, P.O. Box 999, Dept. 17109, Bergenfield, New Jersey 07621-0120.* VISA and MasterCard holders call 1-800-253-6476 to order Penguin titles.

IN CANADA: Please write to *Penguin Books Canada Ltd, 10 Alcorn Avenue, Suite 300, Toronto, Ontario M4V 3B2.*

IN AUSTRALIA: Please write to *Penguin Books Australia Ltd, P.O. Box 257, Ringwood, Victoria 3134.*

IN NEW ZEALAND: Please write to *Penguin Books (NZ) Ltd, Private Bag 102902, North Shore Mail Centre, Auckland 10.*

IN INDIA: Please write to *Penguin Books India Pvt Ltd, 706 Eros Apartments, 56 Nehru Place, New Delhi 110 019.*

IN THE NETHERLANDS: Please write to *Penguin Books Netherlands bv, Postbus 3507, NL-1001 AH Amsterdam.*

IN GERMANY: Please write to *Penguin Books Deutschland GmbH, Metzlerstrasse 26, 60594 Frankfurt am Main.*

IN SPAIN: Please write to *Penguin Books S. A., Bravo Murillo 19, 1° B, 28015 Madrid.*

IN ITALY: Please write to *Penguin Italia s.r.l., Via Felice Casati 20, I-20124 Milano.*

IN FRANCE: Please write to *Penguin France S. A., 17 rue Lejeune, F-31000 Toulouse.*

IN JAPAN: Please write to *Penguin Books Japan, Ishikiribashi Building, 2-5-4, Suido, Bunkyo-ku, Tokyo 112.*

IN GREECE: Please write to *Penguin Hellas Ltd, Dimocritou 3, GR-106 71 Athens.*

IN SOUTH AFRICA: Please write to *Longman Penguin Southern Africa (Pty) Ltd, Private Bag X08, Bertsham 2013.*